Effortless Minimalism: Declutter And Simplify For A Life Of Freedom

GABRIELLE PALMER

Published by Nimzo Media, 2024.

EFFORTLESS MINIMALISM: DECLUTTER AND SIMPLIFY FOR A LIFE OF FREEDOM

First edition. March 10, 2024.

Copyright © 2024 GABRIELLE PALMER.

ISBN: 979-8224338641

Written by GABRIELLE PALMER.

Effortless Minimalism: Declutter and Simplify for a Life of Freedom

Table of Contents

10 Chapter 10: Minimalist Travel and Adventure

11 Chapter 11: Mindful Technology Use

12 Chapter 12: Minimalist Home Design

13 Chapter 13: Minimalism in Self-Care

14 Chapter 14: Sustainable Minimalism

15 Chapter 15: Minimalism for the Mind, Body, and Soul

1 Embracing simplicity for holistic wellness

2 Mindful nutrition and healthy lifestyle choices

3 Finding inner peace through minimalism

Chapter 1: Introduction to Minimalism

Understanding the basics of minimalism

Throughout this subchapters, we will dive deep into the world of minimalism and explore its fundamental principles. We will discuss how adopting a minimalist lifestyle can bring freedom and clarity to your life. So, let's get started!

Minimalism is all about simplifying your life and focusing on what truly matters. It's about consciously choosing to surround yourself with only the things that add value and joy to your life, while eliminating the excess clutter that weighs us down.

Decluttering is a key aspect of minimalism. It involves going through your belongings and getting rid of anything that no longer serves a purpose or brings you joy. By decluttering, you create space for the things that truly matter to you and make room for more freedom and happiness in your life.

There are various techniques you can use to declutter your surroundings effectively. One popular method is the KonMari method, introduced by Marie Kondo. This approach involves sorting through your belongings category by category and only keeping the items that spark joy. It's a powerful way to let go of things that no longer serve you and create a more harmonious living environment.

Benefits of adopting a minimalist lifestyle are numerous. By simplifying your life and focusing on what truly matters, you can experience greater clarity and peace of mind. Minimalism can help reduce stress and overwhelm, as you no longer have to deal with the burden of excess stuff. It can also allow you to save both time and money, as you become more mindful of your purchasing decisions.

Minimalism is not just about decluttering your physical space. It can be applied to all aspects of your life, including your home, work, digital life, and even your relationships. By applying minimalist principles to these areas, you can create a more intentional and fulfilling life.

In the next sections, we will explore each of these areas in more detail and provide practical tips on how to incorporate minimalism into your daily life. So, get ready to embark on a journey of simplicity, freedom, and clarity!

The philosophy behind minimalism

I have always found minimalism to be a fascinating concept. It goes beyond just decluttering and organizing our physical spaces; it's a lifestyle that encourages us to focus on what truly matters. In this subchapter, we will delve into the philosophy behind minimalism, exploring its roots and understanding why it has become such a popular movement in recent years.

At its core, minimalism is grounded in the idea of simplicity. It seeks to eliminate excess and strip away the unnecessary, allowing us to find contentment in the essentials. By embracing minimalism, we can free ourselves from the constant pursuit of material possessions and find greater fulfillment in the present moment.

There are various ways to approach minimalism, but a key aspect is decluttering. Letting go of the things that no longer serve us is an essential step towards creating a more minimalist lifestyle. It can be a liberating process, as we make room for what truly brings us joy and adds value to our lives.

But minimalism extends beyond just our physical spaces. It can be applied to different aspects of our lives, including our digital presence and work environments. By simplifying our digital clutter and streamlining our workflows, we can create a greater sense of focus and productivity. Similarly, adopting minimalist principles in our workspaces can enhance our creativity and reduce distractions.

So, what are the benefits of embracing minimalism? Well, for starters, it can help us cultivate a greater sense of mindfulness. By eliminating distractions and focusing on the present moment, we can experience a deeper connection to ourselves and the world around us. Minimalism can also help alleviate stress and promote a sense of calm, as we navigate life with intention and purpose.

Minimalism is not about deprivation or living a life of scarcity. Instead, it offers us the opportunity to live more intentionally and authentically. By prioritizing what truly matters to us, we can create a life filled with meaning and fulfillment.

In the next sections of this subchapter, we will dive deeper into the world of minimalism. We will explore practical decluttering techniques, discuss the benefits of adopting a minimalist lifestyle, and examine how minimalism can positively impact different aspects of our lives, from our homes to our digital spaces. So, let's embark on this minimalist journey together and discover the transformative power of simplicity!

Benefits of embracing minimalism

Minimalism is more than just a trendy lifestyle choice - it has the power to significantly impact our mental well-being, our financial stability, and even the environment. As someone who has personally embraced minimalism, I can attest to the positive changes it can bring to your life. In this subchapter, I will share with you the numerous benefits of adopting a minimalist lifestyle.

When I first delved into minimalism, I quickly realized how much my mental well-being improved. By decluttering my physical environment and letting go of unnecessary possessions, I experienced a sense of calm and clarity. Minimalism taught me to value experiences and relationships over materialistic pursuits, leading to a greater sense of fulfillment and contentment in my life. It also helped reduce stress and anxiety, as the minimalist mindset encourages simplicity and promotes a more mindful approach to life.

One of the most attractive aspects of minimalism is its potential to improve your financial situation. By adopting a minimalist lifestyle, you learn to prioritize your spending and eliminate unnecessary expenses. This newfound financial discipline allows you to save more, pay off debts, and even achieve financial independence. With fewer material possessions to maintain and replace, you'll find yourself with more money and resources to invest in experiences and personal growth.

Minimalism goes hand in hand with sustainability and environmental consciousness. By reducing our consumption habits, we contribute to the preservation of our planet's resources and help combat climate change. The less we consume, the fewer resources are extracted, processed, and wasted. Minimalism also encourages us to choose quality over quantity, leading to a reduction in waste and a shift towards eco-friendly and ethical products. Embracing minimalism allows us to become more aware of our environmental impact and make choices that align with our values.

Chapter 2: Decluttering Techniques for Minimalism

Strategies for decluttering effectively

When it comes to decluttering, there are various approaches that people take. It's important to find the one that resonates with you and suits your lifestyle. Let's explore some of the different approaches to decluttering and find the one that works best for you.

One approach to decluttering is the minimalist approach. Minimalism is all about living with less and embracing a simpler lifestyle. By adopting minimalism, you can free yourself from the burden of excessive possessions and create a more organized and peaceful living space.

There are several techniques you can utilize to effectively declutter your space. One technique is the one in, one out rule. This means that for every new item you bring into your space, you must remove one item. This helps to prevent clutter from building up over time and encourages you to make conscious choices about what you bring into your life.

Another technique is the four-box method. This involves labeling four boxes as keep, donate, sell, and trash. As you go through your belongings, place each item into one of these boxes based on whether you want to keep, donate, sell, or throw it away. This method provides a clear and structured approach to decluttering.

Maintaining an organized and clutter-free environment can be a challenge. However, by developing strategies and implementing them consistently, you can achieve a clutter-free space. One strategy is to create designated spaces for different items in your home. This helps to minimize clutter and makes it easier to find and put away items. Another strategy is to schedule regular decluttering sessions to prevent clutter from accumulating.

Decluttering effectively requires motivation and commitment. By adopting a minimalist approach and implementing practical techniques, you can declutter your space and experience the benefits of a clutter-free lifestyle. So, let's embark on this journey together and create an organized and peaceful environment.

Practical tips for sorting and organizing

When it comes to organizing, sorting and categorizing your belongings is the first step towards creating an organized and clutter-free home. Here are some practical tips to help you get started:

- Start by gathering all of your belongings and sorting them into categories. For example, you can have separate piles for clothes, books, kitchen items, and so on.
- As you sort, ask yourself if each item is something you truly need and use. If not, consider donating or selling it.
- Use storage bins or boxes to keep similar items together. Label them clearly to make it easier to find things later.
- Consider using organizing tools such as drawer dividers, shelf separators, and hanging organizers to further categorize and separate your belongings.
- Regularly reassess the items you have and declutter as needed. It's easy for things to accumulate over time, so make it a habit to regularly reevaluate what you truly need and use.

Having an efficient organizing system in place can help you maximize your space and make it easier to find and access your belongings. Here are some tips to help you implement effective organizing systems:

- Utilize vertical space by installing shelves or using hanging organizers. This can help free up valuable floor space and make use of empty wall areas.

- Consider using clear storage containers for items that are not used frequently. This allows you to easily see what's inside without having to open multiple boxes.
- Create designated spaces for specific categories of items. For example, have a designated spot for keys, a specific drawer for office supplies, or a shelf for cookbooks.
- Use hooks or pegboards to hang frequently used items such as jackets, bags, or tools. This keeps them easily accessible and prevents clutter from accumulating on surfaces.
- Regularly maintain and declutter your organizing systems to ensure they stay efficient and functional. Take a few minutes each day or week to tidy up and put things back in their designated places.

In addition to sorting and organizing, finding creative storage solutions can help you maintain a clutter-free home for the long term. Here are some ideas to inspire you:

- Optimize underutilized spaces, such as under the bed or stairs, by using storage containers or bins specifically designed for these areas.
- Use multipurpose furniture, such as ottomans with hidden storage compartments or coffee tables with built-in shelves, to maximize storage without sacrificing space.
- Consider utilizing wall-mounted or over-the-door storage solutions to make the most of vertical space in smaller rooms or areas.
- Invest in furniture with built-in storage, such as bed frames with drawers or bookshelves with cabinets, to minimize the need for additional storage units.
- Think creatively and repurpose items for storage. For example, use an old ladder as a towel rack or repurpose mason jars to

store small items like office supplies or craft materials.

Embracing a mindset of simplicity

In this subchapter, I'll introduce you to the wonderful world of minimalism, a lifestyle that can bring immense joy and simplicity to your life. We'll explore various aspects of minimalism, from decluttering techniques to the benefits of adopting a minimalist mindset. Let's dive in!

Introduction to Minimalism:

Minimalism is not just about getting rid of stuff. It's a mindset that promotes intentional living, focusing on what truly matters and letting go of the excess. By simplifying your life, you create space for clarity and peace.

Decluttering Techniques for Minimalism:

The path to minimalism begins with decluttering. Taking stock of your possessions and letting go of what no longer serves a purpose is a key step. Start small, one area at a time, and ask yourself if each item brings you joy or adds value to your life. If not, it's time to say goodbye.

Benefits of Adopting a Minimalist Lifestyle:

Minimalism offers a multitude of benefits for your well-being. By reducing your physical clutter, you'll experience a sense of freedom and calm. A minimalist lifestyle helps you to focus on what truly matters, such as relationships, experiences, and personal growth. It also allows you to save money and reduce your environmental footprint.

Minimalism for Different Aspects of Life:

Minimalism can be applied to various areas of your life, such as your home, work, and digital space. In your home, embrace simplicity by creating functional and serene living spaces. At work, declutter your workspace and prioritize tasks that align with your values. In the digital realm, minimize distractions and simplify your digital devices and online presence. Each area presents an opportunity to cultivate simplicity.

Chapter 3: Benefits of Adopting a Minimalist Lifestyle

Overcoming consumerism and materialism

Introduction to minimalism

Minimalism is a lifestyle that promotes a simplified and intentional approach to living. It involves decluttering your physical and mental space, and making conscious choices about the possessions and activities that bring value to your life. By embracing minimalism, you can experience greater clarity, focus, and overall well-being.

Decluttering techniques for minimalism

Decluttering is an essential aspect of minimalism. It involves getting rid of unnecessary possessions and organizing your space in a way that promotes simplicity and functionality. Here are some effective decluttering techniques:

- Start with one area at a time: It can be overwhelming to tackle your entire living space at once. Start with a small area, such as a drawer or a closet, and gradually expand from there.
- Sort items into categories: Group similar items together to get a better sense of what you own. This can help you identify duplicates or items you no longer need.
- Practice the one in, one out rule: For every new item you bring into your life, let go of one item. This helps prevent clutter from accumulating over time.
- Be mindful of sentimental items: While it can be challenging to let go of sentimental possessions, consider whether they truly enhance your life or if they are just collecting dust. Preserve memories by taking photos of these items instead.

Benefits of adopting a minimalist lifestyle

Adopting a minimalist lifestyle offers numerous benefits for your overall well-being. Here are some of the key advantages:

- Reduced stress and anxiety: An uncluttered environment promotes a sense of calm and reduces visual distraction.
- Increased focus and productivity: When you have fewer possessions and commitments, it becomes easier to focus on your priorities and accomplish tasks.
- Financial freedom: By minimizing materialistic desires and prioritizing essential items, you can save money, reduce debt, and make more intentional spending choices.
- Enhanced creativity: A clutter-free space allows your mind to wander and encourages creative thinking.
- Improved relationships: Minimalism can foster deeper connections with others by shifting the focus from material possessions to shared experiences and meaningful interactions.

Minimalism for different aspects of life (home, work, digital, etc.)

Minimalism is not limited to decluttering physical possessions. It can be applied to various aspects of life to create a more intentional and fulfilling existence. Here are some ways to incorporate minimalism into different areas:

- Home: Create a minimalist living space by keeping only the items that serve a purpose or bring you joy. Embrace simple and clean aesthetics to promote a sense of tranquility.
- Work: Apply minimalism to your work life by eliminating non-essential tasks and streamlining your workflow. Focus on quality rather than quantity and prioritize projects that align with your values.
- Digital: Declutter your digital space by organizing files, unsubscribing from unnecessary email lists, and limiting screen time. Remove apps and digital distractions that do not add

value to your life.

- Social life: Cultivate meaningful relationships by spending time with people who uplift and inspire you. Prioritize quality interactions over quantity, and say no to social activities that do not align with your values.

Reducing stress and anxiety

Clutter is more than just a messy room or a cluttered workspace - it can actually have a significant impact on our mental well-being. Studies have shown that being surrounded by clutter can increase our stress levels and make it difficult to relax and focus. When we are surrounded by piles of stuff, our minds can feel overwhelmed and chaotic, leading to increased feelings of anxiety and stress.

By understanding the relationship between clutter and stress, we can start to take steps to declutter our lives and create a more peaceful and tranquil environment. Decluttering is not just about tidying up, but about creating space for calmness and clarity in our lives.

Minimalism is a lifestyle philosophy that focuses on living with less and intentionally choosing what we bring into our lives. By adopting a minimalist approach, we can create a sense of order and simplicity that can alleviate anxiety and promote well-being.

One way that minimalism can alleviate anxiety is by reducing the overwhelming abundance of choices that we often face in our modern society. When we have fewer possessions and commitments, we are able to focus on what truly matters to us and prioritize our mental and emotional well-being.

Minimalism also encourages us to let go of attachments to material possessions and instead find value in experiences and relationships. By shifting our focus from material accumulation to personal growth and connections, we can reduce the anxiety that often accompanies the pursuit of more stuff.

In addition to adopting a minimalist lifestyle, it is important to incorporate relaxation techniques into our daily routine to promote mental well-being.

One powerful technique for reducing stress and anxiety is mindfulness meditation. This involves bringing our attention to the present moment and observing our thoughts and feelings without judgment. By practicing mindfulness, we can become more aware of our stress triggers and learn to manage them more effectively.

Another effective relaxation technique is deep breathing exercises. Taking slow, deep breaths in through the nose and out through the mouth can help activate the body's relaxation response, reducing tension and promoting a sense of calm.

Physical exercise is also a great way to reduce stress and promote mental well-being. Engaging in activities such as yoga, running, or dancing can help release endorphins and boost our mood, improving our overall sense of well-being.

By incorporating these relaxation techniques into our daily lives, we can reduce stress and anxiety, promoting a greater sense of mental well-being.

Creating more time for meaningful experiences

Introduction to minimalism is a concept that has gained popularity in recent years as people strive to simplify their lives and focus on what truly matters. Minimalism is all about intentionally curating your possessions, activities, and commitments to create more time for meaningful experiences.

Decluttering techniques for minimalism are essential to creating more time for meaningful experiences. One of the key principles of minimalism is to only keep items that bring you joy or serve a purpose in your life. By decluttering and removing the excess, you can free up physical and mental space, allowing you to focus on what truly matters.

Benefits of adopting a minimalist lifestyle are numerous. By simplifying your life and getting rid of the unnecessary, you can reduce stress, increase productivity, and improve overall well-being. Living with intention and purpose leads to a greater sense of fulfillment and satisfaction.

Minimalism for different aspects of life, such as home, work, and digital, can have a profound impact on creating more time for meaningful experiences. In your home, adopting a minimalist mindset can help you create a calming and peaceful environment, making it easier to relax and spend quality time with loved ones. In the workplace, minimalism can help you prioritize tasks, eliminate distractions, and increase focus and productivity. Digitally, minimizing screen time and decluttering digital devices can free up time for activities that bring you joy and fulfillment.

Chapter 4: Minimalism for Different Aspects of Life

Minimalism at home and interior design

I'm excited to share with you some valuable insights about minimalism in interior design. In this subchapter, we'll explore the wonderful world of minimalism at home and how you can incorporate it into your interior design. Get ready to declutter, simplify, and create a peaceful oasis within your living spaces.

Let's start with an introduction to minimalism. Minimalism is all about embracing simplicity and removing excess to create a sense of calm and tranquility. It's not just about aesthetics; it's a lifestyle that can have a profound impact on your well-being. By adopting a minimalist mindset, you'll be able to focus on the things that truly matter and let go of unnecessary clutter and distractions.

Now, let's dive into some decluttering techniques for minimalism. One of the first steps towards creating a minimalist home is to declutter and let go of items that no longer serve a purpose or bring you joy. Start by going through each room in your house and carefully evaluating each item. Ask yourself: Do I really need this? Does it add value to my life? If the answer is no, it's time to say goodbye. Remember, by letting go of physical clutter, you'll make space for mental clarity and serenity.

You might be wondering, what are the benefits of adopting a minimalist lifestyle? Well, there are numerous advantages. Firstly, minimalism can help reduce stress and anxiety. When you surround yourself with only the things you truly love and need, you create a peaceful environment that promotes relaxation and mindfulness. Secondly, minimalism can save you time and energy. With less stuff to clean, organize, and maintain, you'll have more time for the activities and experiences that bring you joy. Lastly, minimalism can save you money.

By being intentional with your purchases and avoiding impulse buys, you'll free up your financial resources for things that truly matter to you.

Minimalism isn't just limited to your home; it can extend to other aspects of your life as well. From your work environment to your digital presence, adopting minimalism can help streamline your life and enhance your overall well-being. By creating a minimalist workspace, you'll be able to focus better and increase your productivity. Similarly, decluttering your digital devices and minimizing your online presence can reduce digital overwhelm and improve your mental clarity.

In conclusion, minimalism is a lifestyle that can transform your living spaces into havens of tranquility. By embracing simplicity, decluttering, and focusing on what truly matters, you'll create a space that promotes peace and well-being. So, are you ready to embark on the minimalist journey? I can't wait to guide you through the rest of this book as we explore minimalist design principles in depth.

Minimalism in the workplace

In today's fast-paced work environments, finding ways to streamline workspaces and increase productivity has become essential. One effective approach to achieve this is by embracing minimalism in the workplace.

Minimalism in the workplace involves creating a clutter-free and organized space that promotes focus and efficiency. By removing unnecessary distractions and simplifying your surroundings, you can significantly enhance your ability to concentrate and get things done.

Here are some key strategies to implement minimalism in your workspace:

- Declutter: Start by decluttering your physical workspace. Get rid of items that are no longer necessary or don't serve a purpose. Only keep essential items that are directly related to your work.
- Organize: Develop an efficient organization system that allows

for easy access to important documents and supplies. Use labeled folders, bins, and shelves to keep everything in its designated place.

- Simplify: Streamline your digital workspace as well. Remove unnecessary files and apps from your computer, delete old emails, and organize your online folders. A clean and well-organized desktop can help reduce digital clutter and improve focus.

- Minimalist aesthetics: Opt for a minimalist design for your workspace. Choose simple and functional furniture, neutral colors, and clean lines. A clutter-free and visually appealing environment can have a positive impact on your mood and productivity.

Now, let's explore the benefits of adopting a minimalist lifestyle in the workplace:

- Increased focus: By eliminating distractions and keeping your workspace organized, you can enhance your ability to concentrate on tasks at hand.

- Improved productivity: A minimalistic environment promotes efficiency and encourages you to work more effectively.

- Reduced stress: Clutter and disorganization can create unnecessary stress. Embracing minimalism can help create a calm and relaxed atmosphere, allowing you to work with a clear mind.

- Enhanced creativity: A clutter-free workspace provides mental clarity and can foster creative thinking and problem-solving abilities.

- Better work-life balance: By streamlining your work environment, you can reduce the time and effort spent on managing and organizing your workspace. This, in turn, can provide you with more time and energy to focus on other aspects of your life.

Incorporating minimalist routines and systems in your work life can have a significant impact on your overall well-being and productivity. Embracing minimalism in the workplace is a powerful way to create a focused, efficient, and stress-free environment that allows you to thrive.

Minimalism in digital spaces

Welcome to the exciting world of minimalism in digital spaces! In this section, we will explore how to create a clutter-free and organized digital life that promotes productivity and focus. Are you ready to dive in? Let's get started!

Before we delve into the specifics of decluttering techniques for minimalism in digital spaces, let's take a moment to understand what minimalism is all about. At its core, minimalism is the intentional practice of living with less. It is about simplifying our lives, both physically and mentally, by eliminating unnecessary possessions, distractions, and commitments.

Minimalism is not just about getting rid of stuff; it's a mindset shift. It allows us to focus on what truly matters to us, reducing stress, improving decision-making, and freeing up our time and energy for the things we love. By adopting a minimalist approach to our digital lives, we can experience similar benefits and create a more intentional and fulfilling online experience.

Now that we understand the essence of minimalism, let's explore some effective decluttering techniques that can help us achieve a streamlined digital life.

1. Start with the Basics: Begin by sorting and organizing your digital files. Delete any outdated or duplicate files, and create a clear folder structure that makes it easy to find what you need.

2. Embrace Digital Minimalism: Adopt the practice of digital minimalism by critically evaluating the apps, subscriptions, and online

services you use. Uninstall or unsubscribe from anything that does not align with your values or enhance your life.

3. Limit Notifications: Take control over your digital distractions by disabling unnecessary notifications. Choose which alerts are truly important to you and silence the rest. This will help you stay focused and avoid constant interruptions.

4. Tidy Up Your Inbox: Implement a system for effectively managing your email inbox. Unsubscribe from mailing lists you no longer find valuable, organize incoming emails into folders, and set aside dedicated time to respond to and clear out your inbox regularly.

By incorporating these decluttering techniques into your digital life, you will create a calmer and more organized digital space that fosters productivity and focus.

Now that we have explored some decluttering techniques, let's take a moment to reflect on the benefits of adopting a minimalist lifestyle in our digital spaces.

1. Enhanced Productivity: By minimizing digital distractions and streamlining your digital tools, you can optimize your focus and productivity. With fewer unnecessary apps and notifications vying for your attention, you can dedicate your energy to what truly matters.

2. Reduced Stress: Cluttered digital environments can contribute to feelings of overwhelm and stress. By simplifying your digital life, you can create a sense of calm and clarity, allowing you to approach your digital interactions with a more peaceful mindset.

3. Improved Digital Well-being: Constant exposure to digital stimuli can take a toll on our mental and emotional well-being. Minimalism in digital spaces promotes mindful technology usage, helping you develop a healthier relationship with your devices and fostering a greater sense of digital well-being.

By embracing a minimalist lifestyle in your digital spaces, you can unlock these valuable benefits and create a more intentional and fulfilling online experience.

Minimalism is not limited to just our digital lives but can be applied to various aspects of life, including our home, work, and personal relationships.

In your home, minimalism can help create an organized and serene living environment. By decluttering physical possessions and focusing on quality over quantity, you can free up space, reduce cleaning and maintenance efforts, and cultivate a peaceful living space.

At work, minimalism can enhance productivity and reduce stress. By organizing your workspace, streamlining your tasks, and eliminating unnecessary commitments, you can optimize your work efficiency and find more fulfillment in your professional endeavors.

In your personal relationships, minimalism can foster deeper connections and meaningful experiences. By de-cluttering toxic relationships, setting boundaries, and prioritizing quality time with loved ones, you can create more authentic and fulfilling connections.

Remember, adopting a minimalist mindset is a journey, and it's essential to approach it with patience and self-compassion. Start small, be intentional, and enjoy the process of simplifying your life, one digital space at a time!

Chapter 5: Creating Minimalist Habits

Developing a minimalist mindset

So, you're interested in developing a minimalist mindset? That's great! Embracing minimalism can bring so much clarity and purpose to your life. In this subchapter, we will explore the principles and techniques that will help you cultivate a mindset of simplicity and intentionality. Let's dive in!

Minimalism is all about decluttering your mind and your physical spaces in order to focus on what truly matters to you. It's about living with intention and letting go of excess. By developing a minimalist mindset, you can create more space and time for the things that bring you joy and fulfillment.

One of the key aspects of developing a minimalist mindset is embracing the concept of essentialism. Essentialism is the belief that by focusing on the vital few, we can achieve more with less. It's about identifying the core elements that truly matter in our lives and eliminating everything else.

Another important aspect of developing a minimalist mindset is practicing mindfulness. Mindfulness is the practice of being fully present in the moment and being aware of our thoughts, feelings, and surroundings. By cultivating mindfulness, we can become more intentional with our actions and decisions, and avoid mindless consumption and accumulation of things.

It's also essential to develop a mindset of gratitude. Gratitude allows us to appreciate the things we have and reduces the desire for more. By focusing on what we already have and being grateful for it, we can shift our mindset from scarcity to abundance.

Now that we have explored the key principles of a minimalist mindset, let's move on to some practical decluttering techniques. In the next section, we will discuss strategies for decluttering your physical spaces, such as your home, work, and digital environment. Stay tuned!

Incorporating minimalism into daily routines

Are you ready to incorporate minimalism into your daily routines? By making small changes to your everyday habits, you can create a more intentional and mindful lifestyle. In this subchapter, we will explore various ways to incorporate minimalism into different aspects of your daily routines.

Before we dive into the practical tips, let's first understand what minimalism is all about. Minimalism is a lifestyle that focuses on living with fewer material possessions and distractions. It encourages you to prioritize what truly matters and eliminate anything that doesn't bring value or joy into your life.

Decluttering is an essential step towards embracing minimalism. In this section, we will discuss effective techniques to declutter your physical, digital, and mental spaces. You will learn how to let go of items that no longer serve a purpose and create a more organized and simplified environment.

There are numerous benefits to adopting a minimalist lifestyle. From reducing stress and increasing productivity to saving money and fostering creativity, minimalism has a positive impact on various aspects of your life. We will delve into these benefits and explore how they can enhance your overall well-being.

Minimalism can be applied to different areas of your life, including your home, work, digital presence, and more. In this section, we will provide practical tips and strategies for incorporating minimalism into each of these aspects. You will learn how to create a clutter-free and intentional environment in every area of your life.

Building sustainable habits

Introduction to minimalism:

Minimalism is a way of life that focuses on simplicity and reducing clutter in order to create a more meaningful and fulfilling existence. It encourages us to prioritize experiences over material possessions and to only keep the things that truly add value to our lives. If you're feeling overwhelmed by the constant accumulation of stuff and are seeking a more intentional and sustainable way of living, minimalism might be just what you need.

Decluttering techniques for minimalism:

Decluttering is an essential step in adopting a minimalist lifestyle. It involves getting rid of the excess and unnecessary items in our lives, allowing us to create space and make room for what truly matters. Here are some effective decluttering techniques to help you on your minimalist journey:

1. Start small: Begin by decluttering one area or room at a time, rather than attempting to tackle your entire home all at once. This will help prevent overwhelm and allow for better focus.

2. Sort items into categories: Group similar items together and evaluate each category individually. Ask yourself if each item brings you joy, serves a practical purpose, or holds sentimental value. If not, consider letting go of it.

3. Practice the one in, one out rule: For every new item you bring into your life, commit to getting rid of one item. This will help maintain a clutter-free environment in the long run.

4. Let go of attachment: Understand that memories and experiences are not tied to physical possessions. Learn to detach sentimental value from material objects and focus on the memories they represent instead.

5. Donate, sell, or recycle: Find responsible ways to dispose of the items you no longer need. Consider donating them to a local charity, selling them online, or recycling them if possible.

Benefits of adopting a minimalist lifestyle:
Embracing minimalism can bring numerous benefits both for yourself and the environment. Here are some key advantages of living a minimalist lifestyle:

- Reduced stress: By letting go of clutter and excess, you create a more peaceful and organized living space. This can lead to a significant decrease in stress and anxiety.
- Financial freedom: By shifting your focus from material

possessions to experiences, you're likely to spend less money on unnecessary items. This can contribute to increased financial freedom and stability.

- More time and energy: With less time spent on cleaning, organizing, and managing your possessions, you'll have more time and energy to devote to activities and relationships that truly matter.
- Environmental impact: Minimalism promotes conscious consumption and reduces waste. By buying fewer items and recycling or repurposing what you have, you contribute to a more sustainable future.
- Improved mental clarity: Clutter and excess can weigh heavily on the mind. By simplifying your life, you create space for increased mental clarity and focus.

Minimalism for different aspects of life:

A minimalist mindset can be applied to various aspects of your life, not just your physical environment. Here are some examples of how you can embrace minimalism in different areas:

- Minimalism at home: Create a calming and clutter-free living space by only keeping items that you truly need and love. Focus on quality over quantity when it comes to furniture, decor, and personal belongings.
- Minimalism at work: Streamline your work environment by organizing your desk, decluttering digital files, and eliminating unnecessary meetings or tasks. Prioritize tasks that align with your goals and values.
- Minimalism in relationships: Cultivate deeper and more meaningful connections by focusing on quality relationships rather than a large network of acquaintances. Invest your time and energy in nurturing close friendships.
- Minimalism in digital life: Practice digital minimalism by

decluttering your digital devices, unsubscribing from unnecessary email lists, and consciously limiting your time spent on social media. Prioritize mindful and intentional use of technology.

Remember, minimalism is a personal journey and there is no one-size-fits-all approach. Take the time to reflect on what truly matters to you and adjust your lifestyle accordingly. By embracing minimalism, you can create a more intentional, meaningful, and sustainable life.

Chapter 6: Embracing Simplicity in Relationships

Cultivating meaningful connections

I'm excited to share with you the importance of cultivating meaningful connections in our lives. Relationships are an essential part of our well-being, and when we nurture them with love and care, they can bring us immense joy and fulfillment.

Building deep and lasting connections requires effort and intentionality. It's about investing time, energy, and emotions into the people who matter to us. Let's explore some practical ways to cultivate meaningful connections:

One of the keys to cultivating meaningful connections is to be fully present and engaged in our interactions. When we give our undivided attention to someone, it shows that we value and respect them. Put away distractions and actively listen to what the other person is saying. Show empathy and understanding, and ask thoughtful questions to deepen the conversation. By being present, we create a safe and welcoming space for connection to flourish.

Meaningful connections thrive when we are willing to be vulnerable with one another. Opening up and sharing our fears, dreams, and struggles allows others to see our authentic selves. It fosters trust and deepens our bond with them. When we are vulnerable, it also encourages others to reciprocate and share their own experiences and emotions. This openness creates a deeper level of connection that goes beyond surface-level interactions.

Expressing gratitude is a powerful way to nurture our relationships. Take the time to appreciate and acknowledge the people who bring positivity into your life. It can be a simple thank-you note, a heartfelt conversation, or a kind gesture. Gratitude strengthens the connection between individuals and reminds us of the importance of the relationship. By practicing gratitude, we cultivate a culture of appreciation and love, making our connections even stronger.

In meaningful connections, it's crucial to be supportive and uplifting to one another. Celebrate each other's successes and be there during times of hardship. Offer a listening ear, provide encouragement, and be a source of comfort. By being supportive, we create a sense of security and trust within the relationship. Knowing that someone is there for us in both good and bad times strengthens our bond and enhances the connection.

Remember, cultivating meaningful connections is a journey that requires patience and commitment. Be intentional in your interactions, and prioritize the relationships that bring you joy and fulfillment. With effort and love, you can build deep and meaningful connections that enrich your life.

Letting go of toxic relationships

It can be difficult to recognize when a relationship has become toxic. However, there are some common signs to look out for. One of the first signs is a feeling of constant negativity. If you find yourself constantly feeling drained, unhappy, or put down after interacting with someone, it may be a sign of toxicity. Another sign is a lack of support or respect. Toxic individuals often disregard your needs and boundaries, and may belittle or dismiss your feelings.

In addition, toxic relationships are often characterized by a power imbalance. This can manifest in controlling behaviors, manipulation, or even emotional or physical abuse. It's important to remember that no one deserves to be mistreated or manipulated.

Letting go of toxic relationships can be challenging, but it is an essential step towards reclaiming your well-being. One strategy is to create distance between yourself and the toxic individual. This may involve setting boundaries and limiting contact, or in some cases, cutting off all communication. It's important to prioritize your own mental and emotional health above all else.

Another strategy is to build a support network. Surround yourself with positive and understanding individuals who can provide encouragement and guidance as you navigate through the process of letting go. This network can include friends, family, or even support groups or therapists.

To protect your well-being, it's crucial to establish and enforce healthy boundaries in all aspects of your life. This means clearly communicating your needs and limits to others and being firm in upholding them. It's okay to say no to things that make you uncomfortable or that do not align with your values.

Additionally, practicing self-care is essential when setting boundaries. Taking care of your physical, mental, and emotional well-being will help you maintain the strength to establish and maintain these boundaries. This can include activities such as exercise, meditation, journaling, or engaging in hobbies that bring you joy.

Establishing boundaries for a simpler life

Introduction:

Minimalism is not just a trend; it's a way of life that can bring immense benefits and simplify our lives. In this subchapter, we will delve into the world of minimalism and explore how establishing boundaries can help us achieve a simpler and more fulfilling life.

Introduction to Minimalism

Before we dive into the practical aspects of minimalism, let's take a moment to understand what minimalism truly means. At its core, minimalism is about intentionally focusing on what is essential and removing the excess clutter that weighs us down physically, mentally, and emotionally.

Decluttering Techniques for Minimalism

To embrace minimalism, it is crucial to declutter our physical spaces effectively. This section will guide you through practical techniques to simplify your home, work environment, digital life, and other aspects of your life. You'll learn how to identify what truly brings value and let go of the things that no longer serve a purpose.

Benefits of Adopting a Minimalist Lifestyle

The benefits of minimalism extend far beyond having a tidy space. By adopting a minimalist lifestyle, you can experience reduced stress, increased focus, improved relationships, and enhanced overall well-being. In this section, we will explore these benefits in detail and inspire you to make positive changes in your life.

Section 4: Minimalism for Different Aspects of Life

Minimalism isn't limited to just our physical surroundings. It can be applied to various areas of our lives. This section will explore how minimalism can be integrated into different aspects such as relationships, finances, self-care, and time management. Discover how setting boundaries in these areas can lead to a more balanced and harmonious life.

Chapter 7: Minimalist Wardrobe

Building a versatile wardrobe

Minimalism is a lifestyle that promotes simplicity and intentional living. By embracing minimalism, you can create a more streamlined and organized life, and one area where this can have a significant impact is your wardrobe. Building a versatile wardrobe is a key component of embracing minimalism and can help you curate a timeless and functional collection of clothing.

When building a versatile wardrobe, it's important to focus on pieces that can be mixed and matched to create a variety of different outfits. By selecting high-quality, classic items, you can maximize your outfit possibilities with a minimal number of pieces, saving you both time and money in the long run.

One benefit of adopting a minimalist wardrobe is that it can help simplify your morning routine. Instead of spending time deciding what to wear, a curated wardrobe allows you to quickly and confidently put together an outfit. This can lead to less stress and more time to focus on other aspects of your day.

Another advantage of a versatile wardrobe is that it helps you to develop a personal style that reflects simplicity and elegance. By selecting neutral colors and timeless silhouettes, you can create a cohesive wardrobe that stands the test of time. This can also make shopping easier, as you have a clear idea of what works for you and what you need to enhance your collection.

By focusing on minimalism in your wardrobe, you can also extend these principles to other areas of your life. Adopting a minimalist mindset can help you declutter your home, streamline your digital life, and simplify your work environment. These changes can reduce stress and create a more peaceful and organized lifestyle.

Tips for sustainable fashion choices

When it comes to sustainable fashion choices, there are numerous ethical and sustainable fashion brands that you can explore. These brands prioritize fair trade, use eco-friendly materials, and promote ethical production practices. By supporting these brands, you are contributing to a more sustainable and compassionate fashion industry.

is crucial in creating a sustainable wardrobe. This means considering factors such as the materials used, the conditions in which garments are produced, and the overall impact on the environment. By choosing brands that prioritize sustainability and ethics, you can feel good about the clothes you wear.

is another important aspect of sustainable fashion. By adopting practices such as reducing, reusing, and recycling clothes, you can significantly reduce waste. Additionally, investing in high-quality pieces that are built to last can help minimize the need for constant replacements.

Capsule wardrobe essentials

Let's dive into the essentials of a versatile and minimalist capsule wardrobe. Having a capsule wardrobe ensures that you have a curated collection of key pieces that can be mixed and matched to create a variety of outfits for different occasions.

In order to build a capsule wardrobe, it's important to identify the key pieces that will form the foundation of your wardrobe. These pieces should be timeless, versatile, and made of high-quality materials. Here are some essential items that you should consider:

- A classic white t-shirt: A white t-shirt is a versatile and timeless piece that can be dressed up or down. It can be paired with jeans for a casual look or with a blazer for a more polished outfit.
- A little black dress: Every woman needs a little black dress in

her wardrobe. It's a versatile piece that can be dressed up with heels and accessories for a formal occasion or dressed down with sneakers for a more casual look.

- A tailored blazer: A tailored blazer is a wardrobe staple that can elevate any outfit. It can be worn with jeans and a t-shirt for a chic and polished look or with a dress or skirt for a more sophisticated ensemble.

- A pair of dark wash jeans: Dark wash jeans are a versatile and flattering option that can be dressed up or down. They can be paired with a blouse and heels for a night out or with a sweater and boots for a more casual look.

- A white button-down shirt: A white button-down shirt is a timeless and classic piece that can be dressed up or down. It can be worn with trousers for a professional look or with jeans for a more casual outfit.

- A neutral-colored sweater: A neutral-colored sweater is a cozy and versatile piece that can be layered over shirts or worn on its own. It can be paired with jeans, skirts, or trousers for a variety of stylish outfits.

These are just a few examples of the essentials that you can include in your capsule wardrobe. It's important to choose pieces that align with your personal style and lifestyle. By investing in high-quality items that can be mixed and matched, you can create a wardrobe that is both versatile and minimalist.

Now that you have identified the key pieces for your capsule wardrobe, let's talk about how to create mix-and-match outfits for different occasions. Mixing and matching your capsule wardrobe allows you to maximize the number of outfits you can create with a limited number of pieces. Here are some tips to get you started:

- Start with a basic outfit: Begin by creating a basic outfit using one of your key pieces. For example, pair your dark wash jeans with a white t-shirt.

- Add layers: Layering is a great way to create different looks. Add a blazer or a sweater over your basic outfit to change up the look.
- Accessorize: Accessories can transform an outfit. Add a statement necklace, a belt, or a scarf to add interest and personality to your look.
- Mix patterns and textures: Don't be afraid to mix patterns and textures. Pair a patterned blouse with a textured skirt or mix a plaid blazer with a floral dress.
- Experiment with different shoes: Changing your shoes can completely change the look of an outfit. Try pairing your outfit with sneakers for a casual look or with heels for a more dressed-up vibe.

By following these tips, you can create a variety of stylish outfits using the key pieces in your capsule wardrobe. The key is to be creative and think outside the box when it comes to mixing and matching.

Now that you have a better understanding of how to create mix-and-match outfits, let's talk about the importance of focusing on quality over quantity in your wardrobe. When it comes to creating a minimalist wardrobe, it's important to prioritize quality over quantity. Here are some reasons why:

- Longevity: High-quality pieces are designed to last. By investing in well-made garments, you can ensure that your wardrobe will stand the test of time and won't need to be constantly replaced.
- Versatility: Quality pieces are often more versatile, allowing you to create a variety of looks with just a few items. They are typically made with neutral colors and classic silhouettes that can be mixed and matched easily.
- Comfort: Quality garments are made with attention to detail

and comfort in mind. They are designed to fit well and feel good, ensuring that you feel confident and comfortable in your clothes.

- Sustainability: By focusing on quality over quantity, you can reduce your environmental impact. Investing in well-made pieces means that you are less likely to contribute to the fast fashion cycle that leads to excessive waste.
- Cost-effectiveness: While high-quality pieces may cost more upfront, they often prove to be more cost-effective in the long run. You won't need to constantly replace low-quality items, saving you money in the long term.

By streamlining your wardrobe and focusing on quality over quantity, you can create a minimalist and versatile collection of clothes that reflects your personal style and lifestyle. It's about investing in pieces that you truly love and that will serve you well for years to come.

Chapter 8: Minimalist Mindfulness

Practicing mindfulness in daily life

Mindfulness is a practice that allows us to fully engage with the present moment and cultivate a sense of awareness and intention in our lives. It involves paying attention to our thoughts, emotions, and sensations without judgment, and embracing the present moment as it is. When we apply mindfulness to minimalism, it helps us to simplify our lives, let go of unnecessary distractions, and live with greater clarity and focus.

Mindfulness can be integrated into various aspects of our daily routines to enhance our overall well-being. By starting our day with a mindful morning routine, such as practicing meditation or engaging in gentle stretches, we can set a positive tone for the day ahead. Throughout the day, we can incorporate mindful eating by savoring each bite, paying attention to the flavors and textures of our food. Taking mindful breaks, where we step away from our screens and connect with our breath, can also help us to recharge and refocus. By bringing mindfulness into our daily activities, we cultivate a sense of presence and create space for greater peace and contentment.

The essence of mindful living is to approach each moment with awareness and intention. By practicing mindfulness, we become more attuned to our thoughts, feelings, and sensations, allowing us to make conscious choices that align with our values and priorities. We can apply mindfulness to different aspects of our lives, such as our home environment, work habits, and digital detox. Minimalism helps us to declutter our physical space, which in turn declutters our mind and reduces stress. By living with awareness and intention, we create a sense of calm and clarity in our lives, fostering a deeper connection to ourselves and the world around us.

Mindful consumption and decision-making

When it comes to our consumption habits, there is often an unconsciousness that guides our decision-making process. We may find ourselves making impulsive purchases or falling into the trap of materialistic tendencies. However, by applying mindfulness to our consumption choices, we can make more conscious decisions that align with our values and bring us greater fulfillment.

One of the key aspects of mindful consumption is being aware of the impact our choices have on the environment, society, and our own well-being. By taking a moment to pause and reflect before making any purchase, we can consider whether we truly need the item or if it is just a fleeting desire. This mindful decision-making process can help us avoid impulse purchases and reduce unnecessary clutter in our lives.

Practicing mindfulness in our consumption habits also involves cultivating a sense of contentment and gratitude for what we already have. Instead of constantly seeking more and feeling a sense of lack, we can shift our mindset to appreciating the abundance that already exists in our lives. This can lead to a greater sense of fulfillment and reduce the drive for constant consumption.

By approaching our consumption choices with mindfulness, we can make more conscious decisions that support our values and bring us greater satisfaction. It allows us to break free from the mindset of constant wanting and instead find contentment with what we already have. So, let's explore how we can apply mindfulness in our decision-making process and cultivate a sense of contentment and gratitude in our consumption habits.

Living in the present moment

Living in the present moment is a concept that is often associated with minimalism. It is about letting go of regrets about the past and worries about the future, and fully embracing the beauty and joy of each present moment.

When we are constantly consumed by thoughts about the past or the future, we miss out on the richness and abundance of the present moment. By learning to live in the here and now, we can experience a greater sense of peace, contentment, and fulfillment.

So how can we start living in the present moment? Here are a few strategies to help you cultivate a present-focused mindset:

1. Awareness: The first step is to become aware of your thoughts and actions. Notice when your mind starts to wander into the past or the future, and gently bring it back to the present moment. Mindfulness meditation can be a helpful practice to develop this awareness.

2. Letting go of regrets: It's natural to have regrets about the past, but holding on to them can prevent us from fully embracing the present. Instead of dwelling on what could have been, focus on what is happening right now and make the most of it.

3. Acceptance: Acceptance is an important aspect of living in the present moment. Accepting the things we cannot change and letting go of resistance can bring us peace and allow us to fully experience the present. Practice accepting yourself, others, and the circumstances of your life as they are.

4. Gratitude: Practicing gratitude helps us appreciate the simplicity and abundance of the present moment. Take time each day to reflect on what you are grateful for. It can be something as simple as the warmth of the sun on your face or the laughter of a loved one.

5. Engagement: Engage fully in whatever you are doing. Whether it's spending time with loved ones, working on a project, or simply doing household chores, give your full attention and immerse yourself in the present moment. This can bring a sense of fulfillment and joy.

6. Simplicity: Embrace simplicity in your life. Clear out physical

clutter, simplify your schedule, and let go of unnecessary commitments. By simplifying your surroundings and your daily routines, you create space for more presence and mindfulness.

7. Mindful habits: Incorporate mindful habits into your daily life. This can include activities such as yoga, meditation, journaling, or taking mindful walks in nature. These practices can help you cultivate presence and mindfulness throughout your day.

By implementing these strategies and adopting a present-focused mindset, you can experience the beauty and abundance of the present moment. Living in the now allows you to fully appreciate the simple joys of life and find contentment in each moment.

Chapter 9: Simplifying Finances

Budgeting and financial minimalism

Welcome to the subchapter on Budgeting and Financial Minimalism! In this section, we will explore the key concepts of minimalism and how they can be applied to your finances. By adopting a minimalist approach to budgeting, you can prioritize your spending, save money, and reduce financial stress. Let's dive in!

When it comes to creating a minimalist budget, the focus is on identifying and prioritizing your needs over wants. By simplifying your spending habits and cutting back on unnecessary expenses, you can free up resources to achieve your financial goals. Here are some strategies to help you get started:

- 1. Track your expenses: Start by understanding where your money is going. Keep a record of all your expenses, big and small. This will give you a clear picture of your spending patterns and areas where you can cut back.
- 2. Set financial goals: Identify your short-term and long-term financial goals. Whether it's saving for a down payment on a house or paying off debt, having clear goals will help you prioritize your spending and make informed financial decisions.
- 3. Create a budget: Based on your expenses and financial goals, create a budget that allocates your income to different categories such as housing, transportation, groceries, and entertainment. Be realistic about your expenses and make sure to leave room for savings.
- 4. Automate savings: Make saving a priority by setting up automatic transfers to a separate savings account. This way, you won't be tempted to spend the money allocated for savings and

it will grow over time.

Now that you have a minimalist budget in place, let's explore some strategies for saving money and reducing financial stress:

- 1. Cut back on non-essential expenses: Review your budget and identify expenses that are not essential. This could include eating out, subscription services, or impulse purchases. By cutting back on these expenses, you can save a significant amount of money.
- 2. Embrace frugality: Look for ways to save money in your everyday life. This could be as simple as cooking meals at home instead of eating out, using coupons or discounts, or finding free or low-cost entertainment options.
- 3. Reduce debt: High-interest debt can be a significant source of financial stress. Make a plan to pay off your debts by allocating extra money towards the highest interest debt first. This will not only reduce your overall debt but also free up more money for savings and other financial goals.
- 4. Build an emergency fund: Unexpected expenses can disrupt your budget and cause financial stress. Aim to build an emergency fund that covers 3-6 months of living expenses. Having this safety net will give you peace of mind and protect you from financial hardships.

Lastly, it's essential to understand and avoid unnecessary expenses. Here are some tips:

- 1. Differentiate between needs and wants: Before making a purchase, ask yourself if it's a genuine need or just a want. By being mindful of your spending, you can avoid impulse purchases and prioritize your financial well-being.
- 2. Avoid lifestyle inflation: As your income increases, it's easy

to fall into the trap of increasing your expenses and adopting a more luxurious lifestyle. However, by keeping your expenses in check and living within your means, you can achieve greater financial freedom and security.

- 3. Negotiate bills and expenses: Take the time to review your bills and negotiate better deals or discounts. This could include renegotiating your internet or cable package, shopping around for insurance quotes, or negotiating rent with your landlord.
- 4. Practice mindful spending: Before making a purchase, pause, and reflect on whether it aligns with your values and financial goals. By being intentional with your spending, you can avoid buyer's remorse and make more informed financial decisions.

By implementing these strategies, you can create a minimalist budget, save money, reduce financial stress, and achieve greater financial well-being. Remember, financial minimalism is not about deprivation but rather about being intentional and mindful with your spending. Happy budgeting!

Identifying and eliminating non-essential expenses

When it comes to adopting a minimalist lifestyle, one of the key areas to focus on is identifying and eliminating non-essential expenses. In this subchapter, we will explore various strategies to help you identify those unnecessary expenses and get rid of them, ultimately simplifying your finances and embracing a minimalist approach to your life.

1. Review your expenses: Start by examining your expenses in detail. Take a close look at your bank statements, credit card bills, and receipts to understand where your money is going. Categorize your expenses into different categories such as groceries, utilities, entertainment, subscriptions, and so on.

2. Identify areas for simplification: Once you have a clear understanding of your expenses, it's time to identify areas where you can

simplify. Look for items or services that you rarely use or don't bring you much joy. These could be things like multiple streaming subscriptions, gym memberships you never use, or excessive takeout meals.

3. Distinguish wants from needs: As you review your expenses, it's important to distinguish between wants and needs. Wants are the things we desire but can live without, while needs are the essentials for daily living. Ask yourself if a particular expense is truly necessary or if it's something you can do without. This will help you prioritize your spending and make better financial decisions.

4. Eliminate unnecessary subscriptions and recurring costs: One common area where people tend to overspend is on subscriptions and recurring costs. Take a look at your monthly subscriptions like streaming services, magazine subscriptions, or even gym memberships. Consider canceling or downgrading those that you rarely use or don't bring you much value. This will free up some extra money and help simplify your financial life.

5. Create a budget: Establishing a budget is an essential step in simplifying your expenses. It allows you to track your spending, set financial goals, and make conscious decisions about how you allocate your money. Use a budgeting tool or an app to track your income and expenses, and stick to your budget to avoid unnecessary spending.

By identifying and eliminating non-essential expenses, you can simplify your finances, reduce clutter in your life, and establish a strong foundation for embracing a minimalist lifestyle. Remember, minimalism isn't about deprivation or living with less; it's about prioritizing the things that truly matter to you and letting go of the excess.

Investing in experiences over material possessions

Investing in experiences over material possessions can be a truly transformative decision. It is a conscious choice to prioritize intangible moments and memories over material goods. In doing so, you unlock a world of personal growth, fulfillment, and happiness.

Minimalism is not just about decluttering your physical space; it is also about decluttering your mindset and shifting your focus towards what truly matters. By embracing minimalism, you give yourself the opportunity to find joy in the simplicity of experiences.

Here are some reasons why investing in experiences is a wise choice:

1. Experiences create lasting memories: Material possessions may come and go, but the memories created through experiences last a lifetime. Whether it's a breathtaking sunset, a once-in-a-lifetime adventure, or learning a new skill, these experiences become part of your story and can be cherished forever.

2. Experiences bring personal growth: Engaging in new experiences challenges you to step out of your comfort zone and embrace personal growth. Traveling to new destinations, pursuing higher education, or learning a new hobby can expand your knowledge, broaden your perspective, and help you discover new passions.

3. Experiences foster connections: When you invest in experiences, you have the opportunity to connect with others on a deeper level. Whether it's exploring a new city with friends, attending a workshop, or joining a community group, these shared experiences create bonds and strengthen relationships.

4. Experiences enhance well-being: Studies have shown that spending money on experiences rather than material possessions leads to greater happiness and well-being. Experiences provide a sense of novelty, excitement, and fulfillment that material possessions often fail to deliver.

5. Experiences provide a sense of purpose: Engaging in meaningful experiences allows you to connect with your passions and values, giving you a sense of purpose and fulfillment. Whether it's volunteering for a cause you care about, pursuing a creative endeavor, or embarking on a personal growth journey, these experiences can enrich your life and give it meaning.

Remember, investing in experiences doesn't mean completely abandoning material possessions. It means shifting your focus and placing more value on the intangible aspects of life. By doing so, you open yourself up to a world of possibilities and create a life filled with purpose and fulfillment.

Chapter 10: Minimalist Travel and Adventure

Packing light and efficiently

When it comes to traveling, packing light and efficiently can make a world of difference. Not only does it save you from lugging around heavy bags, but it also allows for a stress-free and organized travel experience. In this subchapter, we will explore some tips and tricks for packing light and efficiently, helping you make the most out of your travels.

1. Make a packing list: Before you start packing, it's always a good idea to make a list of the essential items you'll need for your trip. This will help you stay organized and ensure that you don't forget anything important.

2. Choose versatile clothing: Instead of packing separate outfits for each day, opt for clothing items that can be mixed and matched. Choose neutral colors and pack items that can be layered to create different looks.

3. Roll your clothes: Rolling your clothes instead of folding them can help save space in your suitcase. Plus, it minimizes wrinkles, so you don't have to worry about ironing your clothes when you arrive at your destination.

4. Use packing cubes: Packing cubes are a great investment for keeping your belongings organized. They allow you to separate different items, such as clothing, toiletries, and accessories, making it easier to find what you need without creating a mess.

5. Minimize toiletries: Instead of bringing full-sized bottles of shampoo, conditioner, and other toiletries, opt for travel-sized containers or consider purchasing items when you arrive at your destination. This will help save space in your bag and prevent any liquid spills.

6. Only pack the essentials: When it comes to packing, less is more. Be realistic about what you'll actually need during your trip and ditch any unnecessary items. Remember, you can always buy something if you unexpectedly need it.

7. Wear your bulkiest items: If you're traveling with bulky items like a winter coat or hiking boots, wear them instead of packing them. This will free up space in your bag and ensure that you stay within your luggage weight limits.

8. Consider your destination and activities: Think about the climate and activities you'll be participating in during your trip. This will help

you pack accordingly and avoid bringing items that you won't end up using.

9. Don't forget travel essentials: While it's important to pack light, there are certain travel essentials that you shouldn't leave behind. These include your passport, travel documents, medication, and any necessary electronics.

10. Practice packing and unpacking: Before your trip, take some time to practice packing and unpacking your suitcase. This will help you become more efficient and ensure that you're making the most out of the available space.

By following these tips and tricks, you can pack light and efficiently, making your travels more enjoyable and stress-free. So, start decluttering and organizing your belongings, and get ready to embark on your next adventure with minimal luggage!

Embracing slow travel

When it comes to traveling, there's a popular movement gaining traction called slow travel. Instead of rushing through destinations, slow travel encourages you to take your time, immerse yourself in the local culture, and create meaningful connections. In this subchapter, we'll explore the concept of slow travel and how it can enhance your travel experiences.

As a traveler, I've always been drawn to the idea of slowing down and fully embracing the places I visit. It's about more than just checking off tourist attractions on a list; it's about experiencing a destination on a deeper level. Slow travel allows you to truly connect with the local culture, traditions, and people, creating memories that will last a lifetime. So let's dive in and discover the benefits of embracing slow travel!

One of the key aspects of slow travel is immersing yourself in the local culture and traditions. When you take your time to explore a destination, you have the opportunity to go beyond the surface-level tourist attractions and delve into the heart of a place. Whether it's participating in local festivals, trying traditional cuisine, or learning about the customs and traditions, immersing yourself in the local culture allows you to gain a deeper understanding and appreciation for the destination you're visiting.

Creating meaningful travel memories is another significant advantage of slow travel. When you rush through destinations, you might end up with a checklist of visited places, but do you remember the experiences and connections you made along the way? Slow travel allows you to build authentic relationships with locals, fellow travelers, and even yourself. By taking the time to connect with people and engage in meaningful conversations, you create memories that go beyond just ticking off landmarks.

Finding fulfillment in experiences rather than souvenirs

I remember a trip I took a few years ago. It was a destination I had always dreamed of visiting, and as soon as I arrived, I was overwhelmed by the beauty and excitement around me. Everywhere I looked, there were shops selling trinkets and souvenirs - keychains, magnets, t-shirts, you name it. And it was tempting, oh so tempting, to want to buy them all as a way to remember my time there.

But as I stood in front of a shelf, filled with colorful knick-knacks that would surely collect dust on my bookshelf, I had a realization. Surely there must be a better way to remember this incredible experience than by accumulating more material possessions.

That's when I started to shift my focus from materialistic travel mementos to lasting experiences. Instead of filling my suitcase with souvenirs, I began seeking out meaningful experiences that would stay with me long after I returned home.

So how can we find fulfillment in experiences rather than souvenirs? Let's explore some ideas.

Chapter 11: Mindful Technology Use

Digital detox techniques

Introduction to Minimalism

Minimalism is a concept that has gained popularity in recent years as people seek to simplify their lives and detach themselves from materialistic possessions. At its core, minimalism is about living with intention, focusing on what truly matters, and eliminating the excess from our lives. It's a mindset shift that can have a profound impact on our well-being, including our digital habits. Let's explore how minimalism can help us reduce our digital dependency and reclaim control over our lives.

Decluttering Techniques for Minimalism

When it comes to minimalism, decluttering is a crucial step in the process. Just as we would declutter our physical space by getting rid of unnecessary items, we can also apply the same principle to our digital space. Start by going through your devices – your phone, tablet, and computer – and delete apps, files, and emails that no longer serve a purpose. Streamline your digital environment by organizing your files and creating a minimalist desktop. By decluttering your digital space, you'll create a more focused and productive environment.

Benefits of Adopting a Minimalist Lifestyle

Adopting a minimalist lifestyle can bring numerous benefits, including when it comes to your digital habits. By reducing the distractions caused by excessive technology use, you'll gain greater focus and productivity. Additionally, minimalism promotes a sense of mindfulness and intentionality, enabling you to be more present in the moment and fully engage with the tasks at hand. This intentional approach to technology can help you establish healthier habits and prioritize what truly matters in your life.

Minimalism for Different Aspects of Life

Minimalism is not limited to just our physical and digital spaces. It can extend to various aspects of our lives, including our home, work, and digital habits. By adopting a minimalist approach to these areas, we can create a sense of calm and order, allowing us to truly appreciate the things that bring us joy. Each aspect of our lives can benefit from a minimalist mindset, helping us prioritize what's important and eliminate what's unnecessary.

Creating healthy technology boundaries

Hey there! Let's dive right into creating healthy technology boundaries, shall we?

When it comes to our digital lives, it's crucial to establish boundaries that help us maintain a healthy balance. Setting limits on our technology use can help us prioritize real-life connections and experiences, allowing us to truly live in the present moment.

So, how can we create these boundaries and foster a healthy relationship with our devices? Let's explore some practical tips:

1. Designate tech-free zones: Designate specific areas in your home or workspace where technology is not allowed. This could be your bedroom, dining area, or any place where you want to focus on connecting with others or engaging in offline activities.

2. Establish device-free times: Set aside specific times during the day when you won't use your devices. This could be during meals, before bedtime, or in the morning to kickstart your day with intention and mindfulness.

3. Create device-free days: Dedicate entire days to disconnecting from your devices. Use this time to engage in hobbies, spend quality time with loved ones, or explore nature. It's incredible how refreshing it can be to have a break from the digital world.

4. Limit social media scrolling: Social media can quickly become a time sink and a source of comparison and negativity. Set a time limit for yourself, and consider using apps that track and restrict your social media usage.

5. Practice digital detoxes: Regularly take breaks from technology to recharge and reconnect with yourself. Use these tech-free moments to engage in activities that bring you joy, such as reading, journaling, or practicing mindfulness.

6. Set notifications boundaries: Disable unnecessary notifications that constantly pull you back into the digital world. Prioritize important notifications and minimize distractions to stay focused on what truly matters.

7. Embrace the power of saying no: Don't feel obligated to respond immediately to every message or email. It's okay to set boundaries and respond at a time that works best for you. This will help reduce stress and allow you to prioritize your own well-being.

8. Engage in offline activities: Find activities that bring you joy and fulfillment outside of the digital realm. This could be exercising, painting, hiking, or meeting up with friends. By immersing yourself in real-life experiences, you'll cultivate meaningful connections and a sense of purpose.

Remember, creating healthy technology boundaries is all about finding a balance that works for you. It might take some time and adjustment, but with each step you take, you'll be reclaiming control over your digital habits and living a more intentional and fulfilling life.

Minimizing screen time for a balanced lifestyle

In today's fast-paced world, it's easy to get caught up in the whirlwind of technology and excessive screen time. While technology has undoubtedly improved our lives in many ways, it's important to be mindful of the negative effects it can have on our well-being. In this subchapter, I want to introduce you to minimalism as a way to minimize screen time and find a healthy balance in your lifestyle.

Minimalism is a lifestyle philosophy that focuses on simplifying and decluttering various aspects of our lives, including our use of technology. By adopting minimalism principles, we can reduce the amount of time we spend on screens and create more space for real-life experiences. Let's explore the different techniques and benefits of embracing minimalism.

Decluttering Techniques for Minimalism

The first step towards minimizing screen time is to declutter your digital life. Start by organizing your digital devices and deleting unnecessary apps, files, and emails. Sort through your online subscriptions and unsubscribe from those that no longer serve you. By streamlining your digital environment, you'll be less tempted to mindlessly browse and spend hours on screens.

Benefits of Adopting a Minimalist Lifestyle

Embracing minimalism can lead to numerous benefits beyond just reducing screen time. By eliminating distractions, you'll find that you have more time and mental space to focus on what truly matters to you. Minimalism promotes a sense of clarity, intentionality, and mindfulness in our daily lives.

When it comes to screen time, minimalism can help you break free from the addictive cycle of constant scrolling and be more intentional with your technology use. By reducing excessive screen time, you'll have more opportunities to engage in meaningful activities, such as spending time with loved ones, pursuing hobbies, or simply enjoying the present moment.

Minimalism for Different Aspects of Life

Minimalism extends beyond just our digital devices. It can be applied to various aspects of our lives, including our homes, workspaces, and even our physical and mental well-being. By decluttering our physical spaces, we can create a calming environment that promotes productivity and reduces distractions.

Minimalism in the workplace involves simplifying tasks, focusing on essential responsibilities, and minimizing digital distractions. By adopting a minimalist approach to work, you'll become more efficient and productive, leading to increased overall job satisfaction.

Finally, minimalism can also be applied to our social lives. By being intentional with our relationships and setting boundaries with technology, we can foster deeper connections and cultivate more meaningful experiences.

In conclusion, adopting a minimalist lifestyle can help us minimize screen time and find a healthy balance between technology and real-life experiences. By decluttering our digital lives, embracing minimalism's benefits, and applying its principles to various aspects of our lives, we can create a more fulfilling and balanced lifestyle.

Chapter 12: Minimalist Home Design

Simplifying home decor

Minimalism is not just a design trend but a way of life that promotes simplicity and decluttering. By embracing minimalist design elements in your home, you can create a serene and clutter-free environment that promotes a sense of calm and tranquility. In this subchapter, we will explore the various aspects of simplifying your home decor to achieve a minimalist aesthetic.

When it comes to minimalist home decor, less is definitely more. Adopting a minimalist approach means focusing on essential elements and eliminating unnecessary clutter. By carefully selecting your design elements, you can create a space that feels open, airy, and uncluttered.

A key aspect of minimalist design is decluttering. Before embarking on your minimalist journey, it's important to declutter your home and get rid of any items that you don't truly need or love. Take a systematic approach, tackling one area at a time, and evaluate each item based on its usefulness and sentimental value. By decluttering, you will not only create a physically clutter-free space but also experience a mental and emotional sense of calm.

Adopting a minimalist lifestyle has numerous benefits. Firstly, it helps to reduce stress and overwhelm by eliminating the constant influx of information and possessions. By simplifying your surroundings, you can create a sense of peace and tranquility in your home.

Minimalism also promotes better focus and productivity. With a clutter-free environment, you can eliminate distractions and fully concentrate on the task at hand. This can lead to increased efficiency and effectiveness in your daily life.

Furthermore, embracing minimalism can lead to financial freedom. By curbing your desire for unnecessary material possessions, you can save money and invest in experiences and things that truly bring you joy. Minimalism encourages mindful consumption, allowing you to prioritize quality over quantity.

Minimalism can be applied to various aspects of life, not just your home. By adopting minimalist principles in your work and digital life, you can achieve a sense of order and simplicity. This subchapter will focus specifically on applying minimalism to your home decor, but you can explore minimalism in other areas of your life as well.

Organizing living spaces for clarity and functionality

Minimalism is all about embracing a simpler and more intentional way of living. It's about focusing on what truly matters and removing the excess to create more space and clarity in our lives. In this subchapter, we will explore how to organize living spaces for clarity and functionality, so you can make the most of your minimalist home.

When it comes to organizing your living spaces, it's important to prioritize clarity and functionality. A clutter-free environment not only looks visually pleasing but also helps to reduce stress and improve overall well-being. Let's dive into some practical tips on how to achieve this in different areas of your home.

The living room is often the heart of the home, where you spend quality time with family and friends. To keep it organized and functional, start by decluttering any unnecessary items. Keep only the essentials, such as comfortable seating, a coffee table, and a few decorative pieces that hold meaning to you.

Consider incorporating storage solutions that blend seamlessly with your minimalist aesthetic. For example, wall-mounted shelves or a media console with hidden compartments can help keep books, accessories, and electronics neatly stored away. Remember to keep surfaces clear and resist the temptation to display too many knick-knacks.

In the kitchen, maintaining an organized and clutter-free environment is essential for efficient meal preparation. Start by decluttering your cabinets and drawers, getting rid of any expired or rarely used items. Invest in clear containers to store pantry staples, making it easy to see what you have and reduce food waste.

To optimize space, consider using vertical storage solutions, such as pot racks or wall-mounted shelves for frequently used kitchen utensils. Use drawer dividers to keep cutlery and utensils organized. Keep countertops clear by storing small appliances in cabinets or using wall-mounted hooks for hanging utensils.

Your bedroom should be a sanctuary for relaxation and rest. To create a clutter-free and calming space, start by decluttering your wardrobe. Keep only the clothes that you love and wear regularly, donating or selling the rest. Consider investing in space-saving storage solutions, such as under-bed storage or hanging organizers for accessories.

Keep your bedside tables clear of unnecessary items, leaving only what you need for a good night's sleep, such as a book and a glass of water. Use drawer dividers to keep your drawers organized and create designated areas for different items, such as socks, underwear, and pajamas.

The bathroom is another area where clutter can easily accumulate. Start by decluttering your toiletries and makeup, discarding any expired products. Consider using minimalistic storage solutions, such as open shelves or wall-mounted cabinets, to keep your essentials within reach and neatly displayed.

Utilize drawer dividers to keep your bathroom essentials organized and prevent them from becoming a jumbled mess. Make use of vertical space by adding hooks or towel racks to keep towels off the floor and maximize space.

By organizing your living spaces for clarity and functionality, you can create a minimalist home that promotes a sense of calm and harmony. Remember to regularly declutter and maintain the organization to ensure a clutter-free environment.

Reducing possessions to enhance living spaces

Are you ready to create a minimalist living environment that enhances your clarity and focus? In this subchapter, we'll explore the process of reducing possessions to enhance your living spaces. By decluttering and embracing a minimalist lifestyle, you'll experience the freedom and peace that comes with letting go of unnecessary belongings.

Decluttering can be an overwhelming task, but with the right techniques, it can become an empowering and transformative process. The first step is to identify unnecessary possessions that are no longer serving a purpose in your life. Take a look around your home and ask yourself, Does this item bring me joy or add value to my life? If the answer is no, it's time to let it go.

Letting go of possessions can be emotionally challenging, but remember that less is more when it comes to creating a minimalist living environment. By reducing the number of items in your home, you'll create more physical and mental space for the things that truly matter to you. Start small by decluttering one room or area at a time, focusing on items that you no longer use or appreciate.

As you declutter, consider donating or selling items that are still in good condition. Not only will this give your belongings a second life, but it will also help you simplify your living spaces. Remember, the goal is to surround yourself with only the things that bring you joy and serve a purpose in your life.

Decluttering your possessions will not only enhance your living spaces, but it will also have a positive impact on your mental well-being. A minimalist lifestyle encourages mindfulness and intentionality, allowing you to focus on what truly matters to you. As you let go of unnecessary possessions, you'll experience a sense of liberation and freedom from materialistic attachments.

Creating a minimalist living environment is about more than just physical decluttering. It's also about embracing the concept of less is more in your home design. Opt for clean, simple lines and neutral colors that promote a sense of calm and tranquility. Remove excessive decorations and furniture to create a more spacious and open atmosphere. By creating a minimalist living environment, you'll cultivate a sense of clarity, focus, and peace in your daily life.

Remember, embracing minimalism is a personal journey. It's about discovering what truly matters to you and letting go of the rest. By reducing possessions and creating a minimalist living environment, you'll invite more clarity, focus, and peace into your life.

Chapter 13: Minimalism in Self-Care

Nurturing mental and physical well-being

Introduction to Minimalism

Minimalism is a mindset and lifestyle that focuses on reducing clutter and excess in order to create a more intentional and fulfilling life. It is about simplifying your surroundings, your schedule, and your mindset to make room for what truly matters. Adopting a minimalist lifestyle can bring about a sense of freedom, clarity, and peace.

Decluttering Techniques for Minimalism

When it comes to decluttering, the key is to start small and focus on one area at a time. Begin by identifying items that no longer serve a purpose or bring you joy. This could be clothes, books, kitchen utensils, or any other possessions. Sort these items into categories of keep, donate, or discard. Gradually work your way through each room and let go of the unnecessary. Remember, decluttering is not just about physical belongings; it also includes decluttering your digital space and your schedule.

Benefits of Adopting a Minimalist Lifestyle

There are numerous benefits to adopting a minimalist lifestyle. First and foremost, it can reduce stress and overwhelm by eliminating the constant need to acquire and manage material possessions. It allows you to focus on the things that truly bring you joy and add value to your life. Additionally, minimalism can improve your financial situation as you spend less on unnecessary items. It also fosters a sense of gratitude for what you already have and encourages mindful consumption.

Minimalism for Different Aspects of Life

Minimalism can be applied to various areas of your life, including your home, work, digital space, and even relationships. In your home, focus on creating a space that is clean, organized, and free from clutter. In your work life, embrace minimalism by prioritizing tasks and eliminating busy work. In your digital life, declutter your devices, unsubscribe from unnecessary emails, and limit your time on social media. Lastly, practice minimalism in your relationships by surrounding yourself with positive and supportive people who bring value to your life.

Streamlining self-care practices

Self-care is a vital aspect of maintaining our physical, mental, and emotional well-being. However, it can often feel overwhelming to incorporate self-care into our already busy lives. That's why it's important to streamline our self-care practices and make them more efficient and effective.

One way to simplify your self-care routine is by prioritizing your activities. Focus on the activities that truly bring you joy and fulfillment, and let go of those that don't. By doing so, you'll free up more time and energy for the things that really matter to you.

Additionally, consider automating certain aspects of your self-care routine. For example, if you enjoy taking baths, set up a bath time playlist that automatically plays soothing music when you start your bath. This way, you can relax and unwind without having to manually select songs.

Another way to simplify is by incorporating multitasking into your self-care routine. For example, you can listen to an audiobook or podcast while going for a walk or doing a simple workout. This allows you to take care of your physical and mental well-being at the same time.

Minimalism is a lifestyle that promotes simplicity and mindfulness. By adopting minimalist self-care rituals and habits, you can create a sense of calm and tranquility in your life. Here are some tips to help you get started:

First, declutter your self-care space. Get rid of any items that no longer serve a purpose or bring you joy. This will create a clean and peaceful environment that is conducive to relaxation and self-care.

Next, focus on quality over quantity. Instead of having a wide variety of self-care products, choose a few high-quality items that truly bring you joy. This will not only simplify your routine but also ensure that you are getting the most out of your self-care practices.

Lastly, embrace the power of simplicity. Minimalist self-care rituals can be as simple as taking a few deep breaths, practicing gratitude, or taking a leisurely walk in nature. Remember, self-care is not about the products or activities; it's about nourishing your mind, body, and soul.

In our fast-paced and consumer-driven world, it's easy to get caught up in the idea that more is better. However, true joy and contentment often come from embracing simplicity. Here are some ways to find joy in the simplicity of self-care:

First, focus on the present moment. Instead of constantly striving for more or thinking about the next activity, take the time to fully immerse yourself in your self-care routine. Notice the sensations, savor the moment, and cultivate a sense of gratitude for the simple pleasures life has to offer.

Next, let go of expectations. Sometimes, we put unnecessary pressure on ourselves to have the perfect self-care routine. Remember that self-care is a personal journey, and it doesn't have to look the same for everyone. Embrace the imperfections and find joy in the process.

Lastly, practice self-compassion. It's important to remember that self-care is not a luxury; it's a necessity. Be kind to yourself and give yourself permission to take care of your needs. By prioritizing self-care and finding joy in the simplicity of it, you'll be able to live a more balanced and fulfilled life.

Prioritizing relaxation and rejuvenation

- Embrace simplicity: One of the key principles of minimalism is embracing simplicity. By decluttering your physical space, you can create a peaceful and restorative self-care space. Start by removing any unnecessary items from your surroundings. Keep only the things that bring you joy and have a purpose in your life. This will help you create a calming environment where you can relax and rejuvenate.

- Choose calming colors: When creating your self-care space, consider using calming colors that promote relaxation. Colors like soft blues, greens, and neutrals can create a soothing atmosphere. Avoid vibrant and stimulating colors, as they may hinder your ability to unwind and find inner peace.

- Incorporate natural elements: Bringing elements of nature into your self-care space can help create a tranquil atmosphere. Adding plants, natural stones, or even a small fountain can help create a sense of calm and connection with the natural world. These natural elements can also contribute to improved air quality and overall well-being.

- Create a sensory experience: Engage your senses in your self-care space to enhance relaxation. Consider adding soft lighting, calming scents like lavender or chamomile, and comfortable textures like blankets or cushions. These sensory elements can help create a serene atmosphere and promote a sense of well-being.

- Set aside dedicated time: Prioritize your self-care by setting aside dedicated time for relaxation and stress relief. Whether it's a few minutes each day or longer periods on the weekends, make it a habit to carve out this time for yourself. Treat it as an essential part of your routine, just like eating or sleeping.

- Explore different relaxation techniques: There are various relaxation techniques you can explore to find what works best for you. Some options include deep breathing exercises, meditation, yoga, or taking soothing baths. Experiment with different techniques and find what brings you the most peace and tranquility.

- Disconnect from technology: In today's digital age, it's easy to feel constantly connected and overwhelmed by technology.

Make a conscious effort to disconnect from your devices and create tech-free zones in your self-care space. This will allow you to fully unwind and focus on your own well-being.

- Engage in hobbies and activities you enjoy: Make time for activities that bring you joy and relaxation. Whether it's reading a book, practicing a musical instrument, or painting, engaging in hobbies can help reduce stress and promote a sense of fulfillment. Remember to prioritize activities that truly relax and rejuvenate you.

- Practice self-reflection: Take time to reflect on your needs, values, and priorities. This self-reflection can help you identify areas of your life that may require more attention and self-care. By understanding yourself better, you can make intentional choices that align with your values and bring more balance and inner peace.

- Nurture your physical and mental well-being: Prioritize taking care of your body and mind. Eat nutritious meals, exercise regularly, and get enough sleep. Engage in mindfulness practices, such as journaling or practicing gratitude, to enhance your mental well-being. By nurturing your physical and mental health, you'll be better equipped to find inner peace.

- Set boundaries: Establishing healthy boundaries is essential for maintaining balance and inner peace. Learn to say no to things that don't align with your priorities or drain your energy. Make time for yourself and prioritize self-care without feeling guilty. Setting boundaries will allow you to focus on what truly matters to you.

- Seek support: Don't be afraid to reach out for support when needed. Surround yourself with positive and uplifting people who support your self-care journey. Joining support groups or seeking professional help can also be beneficial. It's important to remember that you don't have to navigate the path to inner peace alone.

Chapter 14: Sustainable Minimalism

Environmental impact of minimalism

Minimalism has gained immense popularity in recent years as more and more people realize its positive environmental effects. By adopting a minimalist lifestyle, individuals can significantly reduce their carbon footprint and make a positive impact on the planet. In this subchapter, we will delve into the environmental impact of minimalism and explore how it can contribute to a sustainable future.

1.

Minimalism is all about simplifying and decluttering our lives. By having fewer possessions, we consume less and reduce our impact on the environment. When we limit our consumption, we also reduce the demand for new products, which in turn decreases the production and disposal of waste.

Moreover, minimalism encourages us to prioritize quality over quantity. Instead of purchasing cheaply made products that quickly end up in landfills, minimalists focus on investing in durable and long-lasting items. This avoids unnecessary waste and reduces the extraction of natural resources.

2.

Minimalism and sustainability go hand in hand. By adopting a minimalist lifestyle, we make conscious choices that align with sustainable practices. For example, minimalists often opt for secondhand or ethically produced clothing, reducing the demand for fast fashion and its negative environmental impact.

Minimalism also promotes the use of renewable energy sources. By reducing energy consumption and opting for energy-efficient appliances, minimalists can minimize their reliance on fossil fuels and contribute to a greener future. Additionally, minimalists are more likely to support local and sustainable food sources, reducing the carbon emissions associated with long-distance transport.

3.

In a consumer-driven society, we often buy more than we need, leading to excessive waste and environmental degradation. Minimalism encourages us to evaluate our purchases mindfully and choose items that truly add value to our lives. By resisting the urge to buy unnecessary products, we decrease our carbon footprint and prevent the depletion of natural resources.

Furthermore, minimalism extends beyond material possessions to all aspects of life. Adopting minimalism in our digital habits, for instance, reduces the energy consumption associated with electronics and the disposal of electronic waste. Similarly, embracing minimalism in our work life can lead to reduced commuting and paper usage, minimizing the environmental impact of our daily activities.

In conclusion, embracing minimalism not only benefits our lives but also has a positive impact on the environment. By simplifying our lives, prioritizing quality over quantity, and making mindful choices, we can significantly reduce our carbon footprint and contribute to a more sustainable future.

Embracing sustainable living practices

I'm excited to embark on this journey of embracing sustainable living practices with you. In this subchapter, we will explore the principles of minimalism and how they can positively impact various aspects of our lives. Let's dive right in!

Introduction to Minimalism:

Minimalism is not just about decluttering physical possessions; it's a lifestyle that focuses on simplifying and prioritizing what truly matters. By adopting minimalism, we can create more space, time, and freedom in our lives, while also minimizing our impact on the environment.

Decluttering Techniques for Minimalism:

Decluttering can be a transformative process that helps us let go of excess belongings and create a more intentional living space. We'll explore practical techniques for decluttering, such as the KonMari method, the 80/20 rule, and the one-in, one-out strategy. These techniques will help us make conscious decisions about what to keep and what to let go of, leading to a clutter-free and organized living environment.

Benefits of Adopting a Minimalist Lifestyle:

Adopting a minimalist lifestyle has numerous benefits for both our personal well-being and the health of the planet. By living with less, we can reduce stress, increase focus and productivity, improve our financial situation, and cultivate a sense of contentment. Additionally, minimalism promotes sustainability by reducing waste, conserving resources, and lessening our carbon footprint.

Minimalism for Different Aspects of Life:

Minimalism isn't limited to our physical spaces; it can extend to every area of our lives. We'll explore how to apply minimalism principles to our homes, workplaces, digital lives, and even our schedules. By practicing minimalism in these different aspects, we can create harmony, reduce overwhelm, and live in alignment with our values.

Join me as we delve into the world of minimalist living and discover the profound positive impact it can have on our lives and the planet!

Reducing waste and embracing eco-friendly alternatives

I am excited to share with you some valuable information on the concept of minimalism and how it can positively impact your life. By embracing minimalism, you can reduce waste, declutter your surroundings, and live a more intentional and sustainable lifestyle.

Let's dive into the world of minimalism and explore its various aspects, starting with an introduction to minimalism.

Introduction to Minimalism:

Minimalism is not just about getting rid of stuff; it is a mindset that focuses on simplifying your life by removing unnecessary physical and mental clutter. It encourages you to live with intention, prioritize what truly matters to you, and be more mindful about your consumption habits.

Now that you have a basic understanding of minimalism, let's explore some decluttering techniques that can help you embrace a minimalist lifestyle.

Decluttering Techniques for Minimalism:

1. The KonMari Method: This popular decluttering technique, developed by Marie Kondo, involves categorizing your belongings and keeping only the items that spark joy in your life.

2. The 90/90 Rule: Challenge yourself to get rid of items that you haven't used in the past 90 days and don't foresee using in the next 90 days. This rule helps you let go of things that are just taking up space without adding value to your life.

3. The One-In, One-Out Rule: For every new item you bring into your life, commit to getting rid of one item. This rule ensures that you maintain a clutter-free environment and prevent accumulation of unnecessary possessions.

Now that you have learned some decluttering techniques, let's explore the benefits of adopting a minimalist lifestyle.

Benefits of Adopting a Minimalist Lifestyle:

1. Reduced Stress: By simplifying your surroundings, you create a sense of calm and peace, reducing stress levels in your life.

2. More Time and Energy: When you have fewer possessions to manage, you save time and energy that can be directed towards meaningful activities and relationships.

3. Financial Freedom: Minimalism helps you become more mindful of your spending habits, leading to increased financial freedom and the ability to focus on experiences rather than material possessions.

4. Environmental Impact: By consuming less and minimizing waste, you contribute to a healthier planet and reduce your ecological footprint.

Now that you understand the benefits of adopting a minimalist lifestyle, let's explore how minimalism can be applied to different aspects of your life.

Minimalism for Different Aspects of Life:

1. Minimalism at Home: Decluttering your living space and adopting a minimalist approach to home decor creates an environment that is both aesthetically pleasing and functional.

2. Minimalism at Work: Applying minimalism to your work life involves focusing on essential tasks, decluttering your workspace, and simplifying your workflow to increase productivity and reduce overwhelm.

3. Digital Minimalism: With the increasing presence of technology in our lives, digital minimalism encourages us to reduce screen time, declutter our digital devices, and prioritize meaningful online interactions.

By embracing minimalism in various aspects of your life, you can experience a greater sense of peace, clarity, and purpose.

Chapter 15: Minimalism for the Mind, Body, and Soul

Embracing simplicity for holistic wellness

Minimalism is not just about decluttering your physical space; it's about understanding the deep connection between your mind, body, and soul. By adopting a minimalist lifestyle, you can find harmony and balance in all aspects of your life.

When we have too much physical clutter, it can create mental and emotional clutter as well. Our minds become overwhelmed, and our energy becomes scattered. By simplifying our physical space, we create a clear and calm environment that allows our minds to relax and focus.

Similarly, our bodies are deeply connected to our minds. When we live in a cluttered and chaotic environment, it can affect our physical health. Clutter can lead to stress, fatigue, and even physical injuries. By embracing minimalism, we create a space that promotes physical well-being and reduces unnecessary stress on our bodies.

Lastly, minimalism is about nurturing our souls. When we let go of material possessions and focus on what truly matters, we create space for personal growth and self-reflection. Minimalism allows us to connect with our inner selves, explore our values and priorities, and live a more fulfilling life.

Adopting a minimalist lifestyle means simplifying not only our physical space but also other aspects of our lives. By simplifying our routines, commitments, and daily tasks, we can find harmony and balance in our busy lives.

One way to simplify our lives is by decluttering our schedules. We often fill our days with countless activities and obligations, leaving little time for ourselves. By learning to say no to unnecessary commitments and focusing on what truly matters, we can create more time for self-care, relaxation, and personal growth.

Another aspect of simplifying our lives is by streamlining our daily routines. We can eliminate unnecessary steps, automate tasks, and create efficient systems that save us time and energy. By simplifying our routines, we reduce stress and create space for more meaningful activities.

Furthermore, simplifying our belongings and material possessions is essential for finding balance. When we surround ourselves with only the things we truly love and need, we create a sense of peace and contentment. We no longer feel the constant desire for more, and instead, we appreciate and value what we already have.

Minimalism is not just about decluttering; it's about nurturing our overall well-being. By adopting a minimalist lifestyle, we can improve our mental, physical, and emotional health.

One of the significant benefits of minimalism is reduced stress. When we have fewer physical possessions and fewer commitments, we also have fewer things to worry about. We can let go of the constant need for more, and instead, focus on what truly brings us joy and fulfillment.

Minimalism also encourages mindfulness and self-care. By simplifying our lives, we create space for relaxation, self-reflection, and personal growth. We can prioritize activities that promote our well-being, such as meditation, journaling, and pursuing hobbies that bring us joy.

Furthermore, minimalism fosters gratitude and contentment. When we appreciate and value what we already have, we cultivate a mindset of gratitude. We no longer measure our happiness by material possessions but instead focus on the relationships, experiences, and moments that bring us true fulfillment.

Mindful nutrition and healthy lifestyle choices

In today's fast-paced world, many people are turning to minimalism as a way to simplify their lives and reduce stress. One area where minimalism can have a profound impact is in our approach to food and eating. By adopting a minimalist mindset, we can cultivate a deeper connection with our food and make nourishing choices that support our overall health and well-being.

Mindful eating is a concept closely associated with minimalism. It involves paying full attention to the experience of eating, from the flavors and textures of the food to the sensations in our body. By practicing mindful eating, we can develop a greater appreciation for the nourishment that food provides and avoid mindless overeating or making unhealthy food choices.

To support a healthy and sustainable lifestyle, it's important to make conscious and intentional food choices. A minimalist approach to nutrition involves focusing on nutrient-dense whole foods that provide the necessary vitamins, minerals, and antioxidants our bodies need to thrive. By prioritizing quality over quantity, we can nourish our bodies with foods that promote optimal health and well-being.

When it comes to adopting a minimalist lifestyle, it's not just about what we eat, but also how we eat. Slowing down and savoring each bite can enhance our enjoyment of food and help us listen to our body's hunger and fullness cues. Eating mindfully can also reduce stress and improve digestion, as we allow ourselves to fully experience the nourishment that food provides.

In addition to mindful nutrition, minimalism extends to other aspects of our lives. By decluttering our homes, we create a space that is free of distractions and promotes a sense of calm. Minimalism can also be applied to our work environment, where we streamline our tasks and prioritize what truly matters. Finally, adopting minimalist principles in our digital lives can help us reduce screen time and focus on meaningful connections and experiences.

In conclusion, minimalism and mindful eating go hand in hand. By cultivating a minimalist mindset, we can make nourishing food choices that support our overall health and well-being. Whether it's adopting a minimalist lifestyle in our home, work, or digital lives, minimalism offers a framework for creating a more intentional and sustainable approach to how we nourish ourselves. Let's embark on this journey together and discover the transformative power of minimalism and mindful nutrition!

Finding inner peace through minimalism

Minimalism is a powerful approach to finding inner peace and contentment in our fast-paced and cluttered world. By simplifying our lives, we can create a sense of calm and focus that allows us to fully embrace the present moment. In this subchapter, we will explore the principles of minimalism and how they can lead us to a more peaceful and fulfilling life.

Introduction to Minimalism:

Minimalism is not just about decluttering or getting rid of physical possessions. It is a mindset and a lifestyle that encourages intentionality, mindfulness, and simplicity. It is about identifying what truly matters to us and letting go of excess in all areas of our lives. By embracing minimalism, we can free ourselves from the burden of consumerism and find greater peace and happiness.

Decluttering Techniques for Minimalism:

Decluttering is a fundamental aspect of minimalism. By letting go of things that no longer serve a purpose or bring us joy, we can create a physical and mental space that fosters peace and clarity. In this section, we will explore practical decluttering techniques, such as the KonMari method, the 30-day decluttering challenge, and the one-in-one-out rule. These techniques will help us simplify our surroundings and create a more organized and serene environment.

Benefits of Adopting a Minimalist Lifestyle:

Adopting a minimalist lifestyle offers numerous benefits for our well-being and mental health. By focusing on the essentials and eliminating distractions, we can experience reduced stress and anxiety. Minimalism also encourages us to prioritize self-care and self-reflection, leading to improved emotional well-being. Additionally, living with less allows us to save money, reduce our environmental impact, and cultivate a greater sense of gratitude and appreciation for what we have.

Minimalism for Different Aspects of Life:

Minimalism is not limited to our physical possessions. It can be applied to every aspect of our lives, including our homes, work environments, digital spaces, and even our relationships. In this section, we will explore how minimalism can transform these different areas, offering practical tips and strategies for simplifying and finding peace in each domain. Whether it's creating a minimalist wardrobe, organizing our digital files, or cultivating healthier and more meaningful connections, minimalism has the power to enhance our overall well-being.

In conclusion, adopting a minimalist mindset can be a transformative journey towards finding inner peace. By simplifying our lives, decluttering our spaces, and embracing a more intentional and mindful approach, we can create a sense of calm and contentment that allows us to fully embrace the present moment. Minimalism offers a path to greater fulfillment, clarity, and joy, and in the following chapters, we will explore how to incorporate these principles into our daily lives.

Don't miss out!

Visit the website below and you can sign up to receive emails whenever GABRIELLE PALMER publishes a new book. There's no charge and no obligation.

https://books2read.com/r/B-A-WMREB-MFZYC

BOOKS2READ

Connecting independent readers to independent writers.

Did you love *Effortless Minimalism: Declutter And Simplify For A Life Of Freedom*? Then you should read *The Basics Of Feng Shui: A Beginner's Guide*[1] by Margot Read!

The Basics of Feng Shui: A Beginner's Guide provides a comprehensive introduction to the ancient philosophy and practice of Feng Shui. This book is designed for beginners and covers the essential principles and techniques of creating harmony and balance in your home and life.

In this guide, readers will learn about the history of Feng Shui and its benefits, as well as the fundamental concepts such as the Five Elements, Yin and Yang, and the role of Chi. The book also explores practical applications of Feng Shui, including how to use Bagua to analyze and enhance different areas of your space, how to create a harmonious

---

1. https://books2read.com/u/bWYoK0

2. https://books2read.com/u/bWYoK0

entryway and doors, and how to optimize your bedroom, kitchen, and garden for positive energy.

Furthermore, The Basics of Feng Shui delves into specific areas of life that can be influenced by Feng Shui, such as wealth and prosperity, career success, health and well-being, love and relationships, children's spaces, and personal growth.

Through easy-to-follow tips and practical advice, this beginner's guide serves as a foundation for creating a harmonious and balanced environment that promotes positive energy and supports personal well-being and success.

www.ingramcontent.com/pod-product-compliance
Lightning Source LLC
Chambersburg PA
CBHW051802130726

47987CB00003B/1065